THE LAWS OF THE HIGHER LIFE:

THREE LECTURES

THE LAWS OF THE HIGHER LIFE:

THREE LECTURES

ANNIE BESANT

GYAN

Published by

Gyan Publishing House
5, Ansari Road
Daryaganj, New Delhi-110002
Phone: 011-47034999, 9811692060
E-mail: books@gyanbooks.com

Distribution Network
gyanbooks.com
India, USA, Canada, UK, Australia

ISBN: 978-93-6780-423-0 (PB)

First Published, 1903

2nd Impression 2024

Printed at: Gyan Press, Delhi.

THE LAWS OF THE HIGHER LIFE: THREE LECTURES
Author: ANNIE BESANT

THE LAWS OF THE HIGHER LIFE.

THREE LECTURES

BY

ANNIE BESANT, F. T. S.

DELIVERED AT THE TWELFTH ANNUAL CONVENTION OF THE INDIAN SECTION HELD AT BENARES ON 26TH, 27TH AND 28TH DEC. 1902.

BENARES:

THEOSOPHICAL PUBLISHING SOCIETY.

1903.

CONTENTS.

THE LAWS OF THE HIGHER LIFE.

THE LARGER CONSCIOUSNESS.

FIRST LECTURE.

BROTHERS:

THIS year we are going to study together a subject of vital importance to the thoughtful, to the earnest, to those who desire to serve humanity, to those who wish to help the race forward in its evolution. The subject of my discourses I have called "The Laws of the Higher Life," because so many people in dealing with religion, that has to do with the Higher Life, seem inclined to reomve it from the realm of law, and to bring it into some strange region of arbitrary whim, into some strange region of results without endeavour, of failure without weakness. This idea that spirituality is not subject to Law is an idea that is natural at the first sight; for we find a corresponding analogy in the way in which the laws of the physical plane have been overlooked, just in proportion as they have been unstudied and unknown.

We glance for a moment at some sudden eruption of natural forces, some tremendous explosion which throws up perhaps in a few hours a mighty mountain, or we see crags and rocky peaks where before there was verdure, and in a valley which was a plain we discern the outlines of swelling hills. In such an eruption, man once saw something arbitrary, something catastrophic, something disorderly, something unexpected, something outside the orderly growth of evolution. But we know from further study that there is nothing more disorderly in the outburst of a volcano, than there is in the slow growth of the sea-bottom, until at last, after tens of thousands of years, that bottom becomes a range of mountains. The one was thought orderly, the other cataclysmic. But now we know that all natural processes, sudden or slow, unexpected or predicted, all come within the realm of Law, and are utterly orderly in their happenings.

It is the same in the Spiritual World. We may sometimes see apparently sudden eruptions of the forces of the spiritual realm, a sudden change, for instance, of the whole life of a man; we may see the character wholly altered to all appearance; we may see the whole nature of the man changed even in an hour. But we have learned to understand that here also Law is supreme; that in this also there is nothing disorderly, although much that many do not yet understand. And we are beginning to realise that in the spiritual, as in the physical, universe there is the one Supreme Life, manifesting in an infinite diversity of ways, and that that Life is ever orderly in its workings, no matter how strange, no matter how wonderful, no matter how unexpected, they may seem to be to our dim and purblind eyes.

So we shall rest for a moment on the idea of Law, and see what it means. Then after explaining what I mean by "Law," I shall try to show you that, without a possibility of doubt, even apart from religion and religious thought, there is a larger consciousness than that which works in the brain and the nervous system, a larger consciousness than that which we call the waking consciousness of a man. Then to-morrow afternoon, I shall try to show you how that consciousness may begin to unfold and grow by the full recognition of the Law of Duty, by the attempt to fulfil perfectly every obligation of life. In the third and last lecture, I shall pass on to that loftier and sublimer region where the inner law takes the place of the law of outer obligation, where instead of duty, which means the payment of debt, there is sacrifice, which is the outpouring of life, where everything is done gladly, everything is done willingly, in perfect self-surrender, where the man does not need to ask: "What have I to do, what is my duty?" but where he works because the Divine outwelling finds its channel in his life, and he needs no outer compulsion because of the perfection of the inner law. Then he grows by the Law of Sacrifice, which is the Law that rules the universe as well as the hearts of men, the Sacrifice which is a faint reflection of the Divine Sacrifice by which the worlds were made, that Sacrifice which finds its small reflection, its petty minute reproduction, wherever the heart of man throws itself at the Lotus Feet of the Lord of Sacrifice, and thus becomes a channel of the Divine outpouring, however small and insignificant at first, a channel of the life of the Logos, filled not by the little that is given, but by of the great outpouring that uses man as its channel.

Now let us then try to understand what we mean by the term "Law." I have found over and over again confusion of thought on this question of what is meant by "Law," and this lands the student in many perplexities and confusions.

When we speak of the law of the land you know very well what is meant thereby. The law of the land is an ever-changing thing, changing with the change of ideas in the authority that makes the law, whether that authority comes from the mouth af an autocratic Monarch, or from the voice of a Legislative Assembly, whether it is proclaimed in the name of the Sovereign, or of the community in which the law has to act and rule. A law is always a thing which is made, a command issued, and the authority that makes the law can change the law, the authority that creates it can annul it also. Nor is this the only thing that we may observe about the law of the land. The laws are commands: "Do this," "Do not do that;" and the commands are enforced by penalty. If you break such and such a command, such and such a punishment will follow.

Further, when we study the penalties attached to laws in different countries, the punishments for one and the same breach of the command, we find that they are as arbitrary and changing as the laws themselves. They are not the results, in any sense, of the act which has broken the law. But the penalty in every case is artificially attached to the breaking of the law, and it can be changed at any time. For instance, a man steals; one nation will punish that act with the gaol, another with the whip, another with the knife that cuts off the offending hand, another with the rope that ends the life. In every case, the penalty attached has nothing in common with the offence.

But when we speak of the Laws of Nature, we do not mean any one of the things that we have taken as characteristic of the laws of man. The Law of Nature is not a command issued by any authority. It is a statement of the conditions under which a certain thing invariably happens; not a command, but a statement of conditions. Wherever those conditions are found, there will follow a certain event; it is the declaration of a sequence, a succession, unchanging, immutable, unrepealable, because these laws are expressions of the Divine Nature, in which there is no change, nor shadow of turning. The Law of Nature is not a command: "Do this," "Do not do that." It is a statement: "If such and such conditions are present, such and such results will happen;" if the conditions change, the results will change with them.

Nor is there any arbitrary penalty attached to the Law of Nature. Nature does not punish. You have in Nature the statement of the conditions, the sequence of happening, and nothing more. Given such a condition, such and such will follow; the result is an inevitable sequence or succession, it is not an arbitrary infliction or punishment.

But the contrast of the Law of Nature and the law of man may be carried further. The law of man can be broken, but no Law of Nature can be broken. Nature knows no violation of her Laws. You may break the law of man; you cannot break the Law of Nature. The Law remains the same whatever you may do. You may break yourself to pieces against it, but the Law will remain unchanged; you may shatter and shiver yourself against it, but the Law remains firm as a rock, against which the billows break themselves. They are unable to shake it or move it by a hair's breadth; they can only fall into shattered foam at its base.

Such is the Law of Nature—a statement of conditions, of invariable sequences, of inviolable, unbreakable happenings; such is the Law. Thus must you think of it, when you come to deal with the higher as with the lower life.

Then there comes to you a sense of perfect security, of infinite power, of unbounded possibilities. You are not in a region of arbitrary whims, where one day this may follow, another day that. You can work with absolute certainty of results. Your own fancies will not change the Law; your ever-changing emotions will not touch the Eternal Will; you can work with a confidence of result, for you are resting on the Reality, the one Reality which is the one Law in the Universe.

But there is something wanted to work in peace and security in a realm of Law— the thing that is wanted is Knowledge.

The laws which, so long as we are ignorant of them, may toss us from place to place, may break our plans, may frustrate our endeavours, may bring our hopes to ruin, may lay us level with the dust— those same laws, which treat us thus while we are ignorant, become our servants, our helpers, and our uplifters, when knowledge has replaced ignorance. How often have I quoted in this land, as well as in others, those pregnant and significant words, spoken by an English Scientist—words that ought to be engraven in letters of gold—"Nature is conquered by obedience."

Know the Law, obey it, work with it, and it

lifts you up with its infinite strength, and carries you to the goal that you desire to reach. The Law which is a danger when not known, becomes a saviour when known and understood. See how physical Nature has taught you more and more, through the years that lie behind us, this wonderful fact. You see the lightning blaze from the stormy sky, and it flashes down, strikes a turret or a tower, and behold! they fall in ruins, destroyed by the uncurbed and unbridled flash of fire. How dangerous, how terrific, how mysterious. How shall poor man face the fire of the skies? But man has now learned to harness the same fire to his service; he has yoked it by the yoke of knowledge. And behold, the same force now carries his messages over seas and lands, and joins the father to the son who has travelled thousands of miles away, in the loving bond of sympathy and communication; the lightning that destroyed becomes the electric fluid that gives hope and life to the anxious parent, and carries messages of love and good-will over land and sea. Nature is conquered and her forces are our servants, when we learn to work in her way.

So with all other forces, above and below; so in every field of the universe, visible and invisible.

You must know the Laws of the Higher Life, if you would live it. Know them, and they will carry you onward to your goal; be ignorant of them, and your efforts will be frustrated and all your endeavours will be as though they had not been.

I now pass on to speak on what I have called the Larger Consciousness. I want to speak of it to-day, from two standpoints: from the familiar standpoint of the East, which has learned to study consciousness from within, and which regards consciousness, working in the body, as the lowest manifestation of consciousness, a limited representation of the higher and larger consciousness. I want to speak of it, not only from that standpoint, but from the standpoint of the West as well. Chiefly for this reason: as western thought and western science have spread in this country, there is such an apparent certainty about them, such a glamour, that sometimes the western thought will win a hearing, when the familiar eastern presentation of it may miss its road to the mind. I, therefore, want to show you how, among many persons trained in the habits of the materialistic thinking and materialistic science of the West, there is now a recognition that there is a consciousness larger than the brain consciousness, a recognition of a consciousness which transcends the body, and which is a matter of wonder and puzzlement, a matter of controversy and wide-spread dispute, on which men of science are experimenting, which they are trying to understand, which they are trying, as it were, to reduce into some familiar form within the realm of Law. The investigation is leading them, by scientific experiments on the physical plane, to the same results which we find in eastern teachings, results obtained in the East by the practice of Yoga and the consequent development of the Higher Consciousness, that looks from the higher downwards on to the physical plane. Eastern Psychology—starting from the fact of the Higher Self, and seeing that Self working in various upâdhis—traces out deductively its workings on the physical plane. Western Psychology—starting on the physical plane, studying the upâdhi first and then the consciousness in it—is slowly climbing up step by step, until compelled to transcend ordinary bodily conditions, until, by its own artificial methods, it is producing states of consciousness long familiar in the East, and trying in a vague and groping fashion, to work out some theory which will make the facts intelligible and coherent. The long road is somewhat strange and unpromising, but is nevertheless coming to a similar goal to that found out long ages since by the spiritual insight of the Seer.

That is the line along which I propose to travel this afternoon. We need not delay on the subject of what is called waking consciousness—the mental faculties, emotions, etc., that you find around you in ordinary daily life. The West began to study these through the brain and nervous system. There was a time, some twenty five years ago, when no Psychology was considered sound, which was not based on the knowledge of Physiology. The dictum was: "You must begin by studying the body, and the nervous system, and the laws of its working, and the conditions of its activities. As you know those, you will understand the workings of thought, and the activities of the mind; and thus base a sound rational Psychology on your physiological knowledge." I do not think that you would find that idea so completely endorsed among the most advanced students in the West to-day. But none the less, studying along those physiological lines, they came to very remarkable results, as men always will, when they honestly interrogate Nature.

First they noticed that man's consciousness was not restricted to the waking state. They began to study dreams. They began to try to analyse and understand the working of consciousness when the body was asleep. They tabulated the facts after collecting a vast number of them. But they found their investigation was unsatisfactory, because it was difficult to shut out all the conditions that they did not want to study. Sometimes a dream was produced by a disorder in some organ of the body; sometimes it would be produced by over-eating or indigestion. They wanted to eliminate these conditions. Gradually they came to the idea, to try to study the workings of this dream-consciousness by inducing, artificial trance, a trance which would be a dream state under certain definite conditions, which could be produced at will, and which was not the result of the disturbance of any organ of the body.

On this we have all the researches of Hypnotism, experiments repeated over and over again, that you can read in the books specially devoted to these studies.

What was the nett result of these widespread, often-repeated experiments? This: that under conditions in which normal thinking was impossible, because the brain was in a lethargic condition, badly supplied with bad blood, under conditions wherein coma ought to have resulted, an entirely unexpected set of results appeared. The mental qualities did not lessen in power; on the contrary, the faculties of the mind became sharper, keener, subtler, more powerful in every way, when the brain was paralysed. To their surprise they found the memory in the trance state reached back over the forgotten years of life, and gave up incidents of childhood long-forgotten; not only memory, but the powers of reasoning, arguing, judging, all became stronger, more easily used, more effective in their working; under conditions wherein the senses were locked as in sleep the functions of the senses were carried on more effectively through organs other than the ordinary ones. The eye which did not respond to the flash of the electric lamp would pierce distances that in the waking state it did not measure, read books that were kept closed, cut its way through the sheaths of flesh to the interior of the body, and describe diseases which were hidden under flesh and skeleton. Similarly with the ear. The ear could hear a sound taking place far beyond the limit of the waking state of hearing, and answer questions addressed from afar, where the ordinary ear could not respond to the faint and delicate vibrations.

These results made men pause, and they began to ask questions: What is this consciousness which sees without eyes, which hears without ears, which remembers when the organ of memory is paralysed, and which reasons when the instrument of reasoning is in lethargy? What is this consciousness and what are its instruments?

It was not only that in this trance state these strange results came about. It was found that the deeper the trance, the loftier the consciousness. That was the next step. The trance which is not very deep will only show a certain quickening of faculties. Increase the depth of the trance, and the results of consciousness shine out more brilliantly. Facts were collected which showed that man had not one consciousness, but many consciousnesses, so far as their separate working was concerned. They tried experiments with an ignorant peasant woman who in her normal state was dull, stupid and heavy. They put her into trance and in trance she became more intelligent; and what was stranger still, she looked down with contempt at her own consciousness in the waking state, criticised its workings, spoke disdainfully of its limitations, uttering harsh phrases, such as, "That creature," when referring to it.

Still deeper trance, still profounder slumber, and

there emerged from that deeper trance a loftier consciousness, a consciousness dignified, grave, sober, looking down upon both the other manifestations, and criticising them with sternness and separation and distance, criticising their actions, blaming their faults, rising above their limitations. Thus in this peasant woman three stages of consciousness were seen, and the deeper the trance the higher the manifested consciousness.

One other strange fact appeared. In her waking state the peasant woman knew nothing of the second, or the third consciousnesses. For her, they did not exist. The second consciousness knew the one below it, but did not know the one above it. The third looked down upon the two, but knew nothing higher than itself.

Out of this, there came another idea: that not only could the consciousness show higher powers than in the waking state, but that the limited consciousness could not know the larger consciousness which was beyond its own limitations. The higher knew the lower, the lower knew not the higher. The ignorance of the lower was then no proof of the non-existence of the higher. The limitations that bound the lower consciousness could not be used as arguments against the higher condition, which it could not appreciate because of its limitations. Such are some of the results of western science and its investigations.

Now come we to another line of study. Men, materialistic in their thought, studying carefully the mechanism of the brain, came to certain conclusions as to the kind of brain in which abnormal results of consciousness were manifested, apart from all states of artificially induced trance. That School of thinkers may be summed up in the declaration of Lombroso, a great Italian scientist. He declared that the brain of the man of genius is abnormal and diseased. "Genius is allied to madness;" wherever you find brains in which abnormal happenings are seen, you are there on the lines of disease, and the natural goal of that is insanity.

There was some such idea current even before the days of Lombroso, for we know the line of Shakspere:

"Great wits to madness near allied."

In itself this statement need not have done very much harm, had it not reached the length to which it is carried by the School of Lombroso. But as applied there, it became a weapon of terrible keenness against all religious experiences. You find men of this School basing their conclusions on physiological facts, and saying that the brain becomes abnormal, when responding to certain stimuli to which the normal brain does not respond. As that idea gradually spread, they took the next step and said: "Here is the explanation of all religious experiences. We have always had visions and mystics and seers. Every religion contains testimony of abnormal happenings, declarations of visions, and of things normally invisible to the sound, to the balanced, to the rational brain. A man who sees visions is a man whose brain is diseased; he is a neuropath, he is diseased, be he a Saint or a Sage. All the experiences of the Saints and Sages, all their testimony to the phenomena of the invisible worlds—all these are dreams of disordered intellect, working in the brain which had become overstrained and diseased."

Religious people, startled by such a statement, scarce knew how to answer it. Stunned at what seemed to them the blasphemy which regarded all religious experiences as neuropathic, the Saints as nothing but neuropaths, victims of a diseased nervous system, sufferers from obscure troubles of the nerves, they knew not what to say. The idea seemed to strike at the very root of the hopes of humanity, to take away in one fell swoop the world-wide testimony to the reality of the unseen worlds.

There is one answer that might easily be given to this bold statement. I shall make the answer in the broadest possible form, before explaining the conditions under which it may be made.

Suppose it were utterly true; suppose that all humanity's greatest geniuses in religion, science and literature were all and every one of them neuropaths, diseased as to their brains: *What then?*

When we judge the value of what a man gives to the world, we do not judge it by the state of his brain, but by its results on the hearts, the consciousnesses and the actions of men. If every genius were the twin-brother of a lunatic, if every Saint were diseased as to his brain, if every vision of the Supreme and of the Devas and Saints came through a diseased brain in contact with *something*: WHAT THEN?

The value of what these have given us, that is the measure by which we measure them. When a man's life is utterly changed by coming into the presence of a Saint, have we explained the change by saying that that Saint's brain is diseased? If so, then the disease of the Saint is better than the health of the average plodder; the overstrained brain of the genius is a thousand times more precious to humanity than the normal brain of the man in the street. I ask what these men gave us; and I find that every highest truth that stimulates human endeavour and that has come from God to man, every truth which comforts us in our sorrows, which lifts us above the fear of death, which makes us know ourselves immortal, has come from such neuropaths. What care I for the label you fasten to their brains in your physiology? I worship those who gave to humanity these truths whereby it lives.

My second answer is: Let us consider how far there is proof for truth in this statement of the School of Lombroso. I am prepared to admit that, so far as the physiological conditions are concerned, Lombroso is to some extent right; and it is natural that it should be so. The normal brain of man, the result of man's evolution up to the present stage, is the brain which can deal best with the ordinary matters of the world, with buying and selling, cheating and swindling, getting the better of the weaker, and trampling down the feeble. The normal brain of man has to deal with the rough and tumble of life and the tug of the world; it has to do with the ordinary events of life; you cannot expect the manifestations of the Higher Consciousness through a brain nourished on unclean food, made the slave of passions, and the hand-maid of selfishness and cruelty. Why expect from that brain any response to the spiritual impulses of the Higher Consciousness, or any sensitiveness to the keener vibrations of the higher worlds? It is the product of past evolution, and it represents the past.

But what of the other brain, the brain that responds to the subtler vibrations? These are the brains that have the promise of the future. They tell us of the evolution that shall be, not of the evolution that has been. Those who are in the front of evolution are likely, with their subtler more evolved nature, to be far more easily upset by the coarser vibrations of the lower world than those adapted to it; and the very fact that their brains are responsive to the subtler, will render them less fitted to answer to the coarser vibrations of the lower world.

We have two very different conditions to consider; first, the more highly evolved brain, normally sensitive and ready to respond to subtle vibrations, in a state of very delicate equilibrium; that is the brain of the genius—spiritual, artistic, literary. Secondly, the normal brain under stress of keen emotion, rendered thereby abnormally sensitive and tense, and thrown more or less out of gear; that is the brain of the ordinary religious mystic and seer.

The first will be normally healthy and sane, but not well adapted to meet the demands of the lower life, and careless of ordinary affairs; it will be easily jarred by violent vibrations, and hence often irritable and impatient; and it will be more or less easily thrown off its balance. The delicate equilibrium of its complicated nervous machinery will be far more readily disturbed than the rough self-adjusting mechanism of the less evolved brain. Later in evolution, such brains will have gained stability and elasticity; at present, they easily lose equilibrium.

The second, normally unfit to respond to subtle vibrations, can only be raised to a sufficient point of tension by a strain that injures its mechanism and shows itself as nervous disorder. Strong emotion, intense desire to reach the Higher Life, prolonged fasting and prayer, anything, in fact, that overstrains the nerves, will, for the time, render the brain sufficiently sensitive to answer vibrations from the subtler planes of being. Then visions and other abnormal happenings will occur. The super-physical consciousness finds, for a brief time, a vehicle sufficiently sensitive to receive and answer to its impulses. The neuropathic brain does not make the vision; *that* belongs to the super-physical world: but the neuropathic brain affords the conditions necessary for the vision to impress itself on the physical consciousness. Hysteria and other nervous diseases will, in these cases, frequently accompany such phenomena.

It is true that where evolution is understood and wisely guided, it is not necessary that disease should be the condition of these higher experiences. But it is not unnatural that, in many cases, such men and women—unevolved and untrained, with no habit of introspection and self-analysis, and no knowledge of the working of the laws of consciousness, plunged in the ordinary conditions of life—should be less rational on the physical plane than their fellows, caring less for the things of this world because they care so much for the things of the Higher Life.

For a moment let us see why there should be this danger. The reason is simple. Take a string which, when loose, will not give out any musical note. Make it tense, and the note will sound out from the tightened string. It is only when stretched that it will give the musical note. But also, it is then that it is exposed to the danger of snapping. So with the brain. While it is what may be called slack, it simply responds to the slow vibrations of the physical plane; no note of heavenly music can sound out through that brain, because its nervous matter is not sufficiently tense to respond to the more rapid vibrations. It is only when the nervous matter is made tense by strong emotion, or by a great strain of some kind, that the ordinary brain can answer to them. Hence the strain which shows itself as nervous excitement, as hysteria, in daily life, does afford the condition of nervous matter capable of responding to more rapid and subtle vibrations than those of the physical plane. The tension of the nervous state is a necessary condition for the showing out of the Higher Life and Consciousness. When you understand this fact well, the great attack of the School of Lombroso on all religious experiences loses all its power and menace. The disease, the neuropathy, is natural—for you are dealing with vehicles in the ordinary stage of evolution, unfit for subtler vibrations. You have to refine them, to make them more tense, in order that they may respond to higher vibrations. In our present state of evolution, surrounded as we are by unclean circumstances, impure magnetisms, disturbing iufluences of every kind, it is no wonder that the unfit brain, in straining itself to answer to the higher, should be upset by the lower, and become discordant among the rough tones of earth.

Look to the East, and sec how this danger has been understood and guarded against and avoided. Eastern psychology postulates a Self that gathers round him upâdhi after upâdhi, vehicle after vehicle, a Self which gradually shapes his own instruments. He shapes a mental body, that by that his powers of thinking may come into touch with the outer world ; he shapes an astral body, that by that his powers of emotion may be expressed in the outer world ; he shapes a physical body, in order that by that his aspect of activitv may work in the outer world. In eastern psychology, we are dealing with a consciousness which shapes bodies according to its needs.

Now how shall the bodies be shaped to the needs of the Higher Consciousness ? By gradually refining them and bringing them under the control of the Higher : and hence meditation is ordained as the means. But where a man wished to make very rapid progress, it was found easier to go to the jungle and temporarily isolate himself from the lower world. Thus he escaped the coarser magnetisms of the outer world, and put himself in a place in which the rougher vibrations did not reach him ; hence he was less likely to be upset by these harsher and rougher vibrations. There in the jungles and forests such men began to meditate. They made the brain tense and refined by the concentration of the mind, by the gradual restraint of the lower faculties, and fixed it in rapt attention on the higher. The consciousness working from above played on the physical brain through this fixed attention, and gradually made it more tense, and tuned it to respond safely to the higher vibrations. Then it strove to draw the lower upwards, until it answered no longer to the stimuli of the outer world. The same insensitiveness to the outer vibrations that hypnotism gains by artificial means, is gained in Yoga by complete withdrawal of the consciousness from the Indriyas.

The next step, after closing the senses, was to hold quiet the powers of the mind, to make the mind steady, so that it might cease vibrating and become still, able to answer the vibrations coming from above. When the mind was made tranquil and quiet, when no desire was allowed to trouble its serenity, as a lake in perfect calm, on that mind at peace was thrown the reflection of the Self; the man saw in the tranquillity of the mind and the silence of the senses, the majesty, the glory, of the Self. That is the eastern way.

Let us understand from this standpoint how the brain has to be changed, how it has to be refined, and how it has to be improved, how all its connecting links have to be fashioned and manufactured for the purposes of the expression of the Higher Consciousness. Following along this line of self-discipline, or Yoga, what are the conditions of brain evolution? First, purity of body; secondly, refinement of body, and increased complexity of brain. These are essential. Do not suppose that whilst your passions are still ruling you, whilst their demands can upset the mind, whilst the body is unrestrained, that you are ready to receive on the mind the reflection of the Self. You must learn to rule the body, to keep it under control, by giving it proper sleep, and proper exercise, and proper food, satisfying all its needs, so as to keep it in health, not as a master, but as the obedient servant of consciousness. Hear what Shrî Kṛiṣhṇa says:—"Verily Yoga is not for him who eateth too much, nor who abstaineth to excess nor who is addicted to too much sleep, nor even to wakefulness, O Arjuna."

There is to be no extreme on either side; no torturing of the body that is to be the instrument but also no yielding to the body that it may imagine

1 *Bhagavad-Gîtâ*, vi. 16.

itself the master of the Self. Where this training is followed, the brain becomes able to receive the subtler vibrations, without loss of equilibrium, and health is not sacrificed to gain delicacy and sensitiveness. The yogî is most exquisitely sensitive, but perfectly sane.

Having controlled and purified the body, we can make it sensitive to the higher vibrations, responsive to the sounding of the sublimer notes. But to do this, we must lose our interest in the lower, and become indifferent to the attractions of the outer life. Vairâgya, dispassion, we must have, for that is a condition of the Higher Consciousness revealing itself in the lower world. While you love the lower things of the world, the Higher Consciousness cannot use this upâdhi as its vehicle. One-pointed devotion to the Supreme, a clear, well-balanced, intelligent development of the intellect and emotions, this is the road along which we must tread, if the Higher Consciousness is to be manifested on earth. We must be pure in life, compassionate, and tender; we must learn to see the Self in every one around us, in the ugly as well as in the beautiful, in the low as well as in the high, in the plant as well as in the Deva. He who sees the Self in everything, and all things in the Self, he seeth, verily, he seeth.

——:O:——

Second Lecture.

THE LAW OF DUTY.

BROTHERS :

IN our talk of yesterday, we came to certain definite conclusions. We studied the nature of Law, and we found that a larger Consciousness than the waking brain consciousness of man exists in each of us. We saw that if that Consciousness was to manifest itself, then it was necessary that the senses should be utterly controlled, and the mind should be under restraint. So far we went in our study of the Higher Life yesterday.

Now we enter on another stage of our study, and we have to consider how a man should guide his conduct, in order that in him the Higher Consciousness may manifest itself in all its power. We want to see the stages of the preparation and to realise what each of us can do, now in the position that we are, to prepare ourselves for that divine unfolding, for that blossoming of the bud of Consciousness, which is growing slowly within each of us. And in order that we may follow the subject well, let us define one or two words and expressions that we shall have to use throughout.

First, what is meant by the Higher Life? I have used it in the widest sense of the term, for all manifestations of life above the physical. It would include the manifestation of man in the various worlds invisible to the eyes of the flesh—regions of which we speak by using the word "planes"—astral plane, mânasic plane, buddhic plane, atmic plane, and whatever in the vast universe may lie beyond.

What do we mean by "spiritual"? All manifestations of the Higher Life as thus defined are not necessarily spiritual. We must separate, in our thought, the form in which Consciousness is embodied and the Consciousness itself. Nothing that is of the form is spiritual in its nature. The life of form on every plane belongs to the prâkritic manifestation, and not to the spiritual. The manifestation of the life in form may be on the astral plane, or on the mânasic plane, but it is no more spiritual there than it is on the physical plane.

Everywhere the prâkritic manifestation is purely phenomenal, and nothing that is phenomenal can be said to be spiritual. That is a matter to be remembered. Otherwise we shall blunder sorely in our studies, and we shall not choose rightly the means by which the spiritual is to evolve. It matters not whether the life of form be lived on a lower or a higher plane—stone, vegetable, animal, man or Deva. In so far as it is prâkritic, phenomenal, in its nature, it has nothing to do with that which can claim the name of the Spiritual. A man may develop astral or mânasic Siddhis, he may possess an eye that can see far into space, far abroad over the universe, he may hear the singing of the Devas and listen to the chanting in Svarga, but all that is phenomenal, all that is transitory. The Spiritual and the Eternal is not of the life of form.

What then is the Spiritual? It is alone the life of the Consciousness which recognises Unity, which sees one Self in everything and everything in the Self. The spiritual life is the life which looking into the infinite number of phenomena, pierces through the veil of Mâyâ and sees the One and the Eternal within each changing form. To know the Self, to love the Self, to realise the Self, that and that alone is Spirituality, even as to see the Self everywhere alone is Wisdom. All outside that is ignorance; all outside that is unspiritual. If once you understand this definition, you will find yourself compelled to choose not the phenomenal but the real, to choose the life of the Spirit as distinguished from the life of the form, though on the highest plane. You will be compelled to choose definite methods for evolving the life of the Spirit, and you will search for the knowledge of the law which shall enable the Consciousness to unfold, so that it may recognise its unity with all Consciousnesses everywhere, so that every form shall be dear not for the sake of the form but for the sake of the Self, which is the life and reality of the form. Remember how Yâjñavalkya taught Maitreyî, when she desired to know this same spiritual part of the Higher Life, and he said: "Not for the sake of the husband is the husband dear, but for the sake of the Self is the husband dear; not for the sake of the wife is the wife dear, but for the sake of the Self is the wife dear;" and so on from one thing to another, to child, lover, friend, ending at last with the life that stretches beyond the physical: "Not for the sake of the Devas are the Devas dear, but for the sake of the Self the Devas are dear."

That is the note of the Spirit. All is in the

Self. The One is recognised everywhere. How shall we attain it, how shall we, blinded by matter, know it?

Note that the first great step towards the attainment of this realisation is the Law of Duty. Let us pause a moment to understand why the Law of Duty is the first truth which a man must obey, if he wishes to rise to the spiritual life. You find beings around us, belonging to the higher worlds, who are not spiritual, but who exercise enormous forces, who energise nature, bending matter to their will: mighty beings of tremendous power who range the world around us, some helping forward evolution by inspiring noble thought and high endeavour; others who are also helping forward evolution, but who do it by striving to hinder the progress of man and to bewilder him, in order that man may learn to plant his foot firmly, and by struggling against the wrong may become perfect in the right. Both these sides are of the divine manifestation; you cannot have the light without the darkness, nor progress without resistance; there is no evolution without the force that works against it. It is the force that works against evolution that gives stability to progress, and makes possible the higher growth of man. We must however beware that we do not fall into the common error and confuse the functions of the two. The forces and the beings of the higher world who help evolution forward, who guide and inspire, lift and purify us, these are rightly the objects of reverence, and in their steps we may safely tread, and to them we may safely pray. The other powers are our friends, in so far as we resist them and oppose them: and they can only help us then when we strive against them. For then they strengthen the spiritual muscles and nerves. But the success that we can gain in their region in evolution lies in the power by which we combat them; and the strength that is evolved in the struggle helps forward our evolution. They are not to be followed and not to be obeyed, not to be meditated upon, nor appealed to. How then shall the wayfarer choose his path, and know the test whereby one may be distinguished from the other?

By the Law of Duty within him, by the divine Self which points out the path of progress, by obedience to Duty above all else, and by reverencing Truth as greatest, and worshipping it without a shadow of wavering, or an idea of change.

Now it is sometime said, and it is true, that in the Samskrit tongue there is no word for what in the West has been called Conscience. Taking the testimony of Samskrit scholars, we learn that there is not a word which is the exact equivalent of Conscience. But we are not looking for words but for things, not searching for labels but for facts. I ask you in what Scriptures, or in what literature, you can find better expression of this idea of Conscience, than in the Eastern, where we find obedience to Conscience and reverence for Duty shining out in golden example and practice in the lives of men of ancient India, as well as in the precepts recorded in ancient Samskrit books.

Take for example the conduct of Yudhiṣhṭhira, the righteous King, who once in a trial at the hands of Shrî Kṛiṣhṇa Himself had fallen from truth. See him in the last scene of his life, ere he leaves this earth, when Indra the King of the Devas comes down and bids him mount his car and go to the highest heaven. Remember how, pointing to the faithful dog that had survived the terrible journey across the great desert, he says: "My heart is moved with compassion for the hound; let him come to Svarga with me." "There is no place for dogs in Svarga," replies Indra; and as Yudhiṣhṭhira still refused he grew sarcastic, saying: "You let your brothers die in the great desert; you left them lying dead. You left Draupadî dying, and her corpse did not check your forward course. If brothers and wife were left behind, why cling to a dog, and why wish to take him onward?" Then replied Yudhiṣhṭhira: "For the dead we can do nothing; I could not help my brothers or my wife. But this creature is alive, and is not dead. Equal to the killing of the twice-born, equal to the spoiling of the goods of the Brâhmaṇa, is the sin of deserting a helpless one, who has taken refuge with you. I will not go to Heaven alone." And when he was found unshaken by divine argument, and by all appeals of Deva sophistry, then the dog vanished, and Dharma incarnate rose up before him, and bade him to mount to heaven. Stronger than command of Indra was the steadfast conscience of the king. No lure of immortality made him swerve from duty, nor could the sweet tongue of the Deva blind him as to the path of righteousness to which his conscience pointed.

Now come further back in evolution with me, and see where Bali, King of Daityas, is offering sacrifice to the Supreme; a misshapen dwarf comes up and begs a boon: "Three steps of earth, O King, as sacrificial gift." Three steps of earth, measured by those short limbs of the dwarf? a petty gift, in truth. The boon is granted; and lo! the first step covers earth; the second spans the sky; where shall the third step be planted? The earth and sky are covered; what then remains?

There is but the breast of the devotee, who throws himself down, in order that the third step may be planted upon his bosom. Then come remonstrances from every side: "It is fraud." "It is deception." "It is Hari Himself who is luring thee to thy destruction. Break thy word, and do not follow truth to ruin." But although the voices strike his ear, he thinks truth and duty and conscience greater than loss of life and kingdom, and lies prone, unmoved. Presently his Guru comes, than whom none may be more revered, and the Guru bids him break his word; and when even to him Bali listens not, the Guru curses him for his disobedience—and then? Then the form of Viṣhṇu is manifest, that mighty form which covers earth and sky, and a voice, speaking with the sweetness of the cooing of the dove, is heard in the silence that prevails: "Bali, defeated and attacked on all sides, reviled by his friends, cursed by his preceptor, this Bali will not give up truth." Then Viṣhṇu declares that he, in a future Kalpa, will be Indra, the monarch of the Devas, for only where truth is worshipped may power safely be entrusted.

With such cases before us and scores of others might be cited, what matters it that no one word for "conscience" is found? The idea shines forth constantly, me idea of fidelity to duty, the recognition of the Law of Duty. And what is the one word which is the key-note of the Hindu people? It is Dharma, and this is duty, righteousness.

What is then the Law of Duty? It varies with every stage of evolution, though the principle is ever the same. It is progressive, as evolution is progressive. The duty of the savage is not the duty of the cultured and evolved man. The duty of the teacher is not the duty of the King. The duty of the merchant is not the duty of the warrior. So that when we are studying the Law of Duty, we must begin by studying our own place on the great ladder of evolution, by studying the circumstances around us that show our karma, by studying our own powers and capacities, and ascertaining our weaknesses. And out of this careful study we must find out the Law of Duty by which we must guide our steps.

Dharma is the same for all who are in the same stage of evolution and the same circumstances, and there is some Dharma common for all. There are duties laid down for all. The tenfold duties laid down by Manu are binding for all who would work with evolution, the general duties that man owes to man. The experience of the past has marked them out, and no doubt can arise about them.

But there are many questions of Dharma that

are not so simple in their character. The real difficulty of those who are striving to advance along the path of spirituality is often to distinguish their Dharma, and to know what the Law of Duty demands.

There are many cases in our experience, day after day, in which conflict of duties appears to arise. One duty calls us one way, and another duty another way. Then we find ourselves perplexed as to Dharma, as Arjuna was perplexed on Kurukshetra.

These are some of the difficulties of the Higher Life, the tests of evolving Consciousness. It is little difficult to perform the duty that is clear and simple. Blunder is not likely to occur there. But when the path of action is tangled, when we cannot see, how then shall we tread our doubtful way through the darkness? Some dangers we know which cloud the reason and the vision, and make it hard to distinguish duty. Our personalities are our ever present foes, that lower self which clothes itself in a hundred different forms, which sometimes puts on the very mask of Dharma, and so prevents our recognising that, in following it, we are following the path of desire rather than the path of duty. How are we then to distinguish when the personality is controlling us, and when duty directs? How shall we know when we are misled, when the very atmosphere of personality which encircles us distorts the object beyond it by desire and passion?

I know of no safer way in such trials, than to retire quietly into the chamber of the heart, to try to put personal desires aside, to strive to separate ourself for a moment from the personality, and look at the question in a broader, clearer light, with prayer to our Gurudeva to guide us; then, in such light as we may win by prayer, self-analysis and meditation, to choose the path which appears to us to be the path of duty. We may blunder; but if we blunder, having striven to see clearly, then let us remember that the mistake is necessary in order to teach us a lesson, which it is vital for our progress that we should learn: we may blunder, and choose the path of desire, misled by its influence, and when we think we are choosing Dharma, we may be moved by Ahamkâra. Even if that be so, we have done rightly in struggling to see the right, and in resolving to do the right. Even if in striving to do the right, we do the wrong, we may rest assured that the God within us will correct us. Why should we despair because we make mistakes, when our heart is fixed on the Supreme, when we are striving to see the right? Nay, rather, when we have striven to do the right and have done the wrong in our blindness, we will welcome the pain that clears the mental vision, and we will cry undaunted to the Lord of the burning-ghat: "Send down yet again Thy flames to burn out everything that obstructs the vision, all dross that is mixed with the pure gold; burn Thou, O Radiant One, till we come out from the fire as pure and refined gold, whence all impurities have vanished."

But if we, coward-like, shrinking from the responsibility of coming to a decision, and deaf to the voice of conseience, choose the easy path which another may tell us is the right one but which we feel to be wrong, and thus, against our own conscience, follow another's path, what have we done? We have dulled the divine voice within us; we have chosen the lower rather than the higher; we have chosen the easy and not the difficult; we have chosen the surrender of the will rather than its purification; and even though the path that we tread by another's choice may be the better path of the two, we have none the less injured our evolution by our failure to do that which we believed to be right. That mistake is a thousand-fold more injurious than blundering through the glamour of desire. To do what we believe to be the highest—that is the only safe path for the spiritual aspirant. If you affront your sense of right by taking that as right which in your heart you feel to be wrong, standing on another's advice and command, then you lose the very power to distinguish between right and wrong, and you put out the only light you have, however poor that light may be, and you choose to walk in darkness rather than in twilight. How will you be able to distinguish between light and dark, between the White Brothers and the Black, how will you know that this is divine and that is âsuric, how will you discern the Deva from the Asura, unless you test them by the standard of duty, and by the righteousness they incarnate? Where duty is not done, where love, compassion, purity, self-sacrifice, are not seen, there there may be power, but there there is not the spirituality which enlightens the world, and sets an example to men.

In the path of spiritual aspiration, we must not expect to find the way easy and plain ; for the spiritual life is not obtained save by repeated endeavour and constant failure, and the path of duty is not found but by undaunted perseverance. Let us but desire to know the right, and we shall surely know it, no matter by what path of anguish the right is to be found. In our daily life, let us practise to do the right, as far as we see it, and we shall surely see more clearly as we proceed.

But since many become confused as to the guides who may aid them in their upward treading, and as to how they may know such guides, let us pause and see what are the tests and proofs of spiritual life, of the spirituality which is to be copied, to be lived, which is an example, a light, in the world.

The test and proof of the advanced spiritual man, fit to be the guide, the teacher, the helper of others, is in the perfection of the qualities that the aspirant is striving to produce in himself. He performs perfectly what the aspirant performs imperfectly; he incarnates the ideal which the aspirant is striving to reproduce. What then are these qualities, which mark the spiritual life?

Around us on every side we see men and women seeking for light, struggling for growth, puzzled, confused, bewildered.

To all and each one that we meet, we owe a duty. No one who comes within the circle of our life, but we have a duty towards that person. The world is not ruled by chance; no fortuitous happenings come into the lives of men. Duties are obligations we owe to those around us; and every-one within our circle is one to whom we owe a duty. What is the duty that we owe to each It is the definite payment of those debts with which we are familiar in our studies; the duty of reverencing and obeying those who are superior to us, who are above us; the duty of being gentle and affectionate and helpful to those around us, on our own level; the duty of protection, kindness, helpfulness and compassion to those below us. These are universal duties, and no aspirant should fail in the attempt at least to fulfil them; without the fulfilment of these there is no spiritual life.

But even when we have discharged to the utmost the debts enjoined by the letter of the law; when we have paid and fulfilled the obligations imposed by our birth, by our family ties, by our social surroundings and national karma; there still remains one higher duty which we may place before us as the light to illumine our path.

Whenever a person comes within our circle of life, let us look to it that he leaves that circle a better man, the better for his contact with us. When an ignorant person comes and we have knowledge, let him leave us a better-informed man. When a sorrowful person comes to us, let him leave us a little less sorrowful, for our having shared the sorrow with him. When a helpless person comes and we are strong, let him leave us strengthened by our strength and not humiliated by our pride. Everywhere let us be tender and patient, gentle and helpful with all. Do not let us in our daily path be harsh, so as to confuse, bewilder and perplex others. There is enough of sorrow in the world. Let the spiritual man be a source of comfort and of peace; let him be as a light in the world, so that all may walk more safely when they come within the circle of his influence. Let us judge our spirituality by our effect on the world, and let us be careful that the world may grow purer, better, happier, because we are living in it.

What are we here for, save to help each other, to love each other, to uplift each other? Is the spiritual man to hinder or to uplift his fellowmen? Is he to be a Saviour of mankind, or one who throws back the evolution of his fellows, from whom one goes away discouraged? Watch how your influence affects others: be careful how your words affect their lives. Your tongue must be gentle, your words must be loving; no slander, gossip, or harshness of speech, or suspicion of unkind motive, must pollute the lips that are striving to be the vehicle of spiritual life. The difficulty is in us and not outside of us. It is here in our own lives and our own conduct that the spiritual evolution must be made. Help your brothers, and do not be harsh with them. Lift them up when they fall, and remember, if you stand to-day, you too may fall to-morrow, and may need the helping hand of another, in order that you may rise.

Every scripture declares that the Heart of the Divine Life is Infinite Compassion. Compassionate then must be the spiritual man. Let us, in our poor measure, in our tiny cups of love, give to our fellow man one drop of that ocean of compassion in which the universe is bathed. You never can be wrong in helping your brother, and in putting your own needs behind the supplying of his wants.

That and that alone is true spirituality, and it means coming back to the point from which we started. It means the recognition of one Self in all. The spiritual man must lead a higher life than the life of altruism. He must lead the life of self-identification with all that lives and moves. There is no "other" in this world: we all are one. Each is a separate form, but one Spirit moves and lives in all.

Listen to what spoke the Divine Love, Shrī Kṛiṣhṇa, when looking over the world of men, He passed His Divine verdict on the righteous and the sinful. "If the most sinful worship me," said He, "with undivided heart, he too must be accounted righteous, for he hath rightly resolved; speedily he becometh dutiful and goeth to eternal peace. O Kaunteya, know thou certainly that My devotee perisheth never."

Resolve rightly, then, and no fear need enter your heart. You may blunder, you may make errors, you may fall over and over again, but speedily you will become dutiful, and go to Eternal Peace.

Let us give devotion, then, to the Supreme Love. Let us recognise our one-ness in Him, and therefore our one-ness with each other; and because we have rightly resolved, though we have weaknesses and faults, there is the promise of Truth Itself, speedily we shall become dutiful and go to Peace.

---

* *Bhagavad-Gîtâ*. ix. 30, 31.

Lecture Third.

THE LAW OF SACRIFICE.

BROTHERS:

WE have already seen that a man can only realise himself as a Higher Consciousness in proportion as he tranquillises the senses, in proportion as he restrains the mind. We have then seen that he advances towards the realisation of the Higher Life in proportion as he obeys the Law of Duty, as he definitely and resolutely sets himself to the payment of the obligations that he has incurred.

To-night we shall try to rise into a higher region, and see how, after he has practised the Law of Duty, the Law of Sacrifice lifts him upwards and enables him to reach union with the Divine. It is the Law of Sacrifice that we are now to study.

It has often been said and truly said, that sacrifice is printed on the universe in which we live.

And why should it not be so, since the universe in which we live itself originates in an act of sacrifice, in the limitation of the Logos in order that the world may come forth. All the religions have on this point but a single teaching, that manifestation began by an act of Divine Sacrifice. Each Scripture may in turn be quoted to prove the point, but it is so familiar to all of you that no proof is needed.

The nature of that sacrifice is seen by us as consisting in this assumption of the limitations of matter by the Immaterial, in the veiling of the Unconditioned in conditions, in the binding of the Free within bonds. The first thought that we have, as we watch the evolving of a universe, is that this manifestation of life is only possible by its limitations, that these mark out the conditions of its evolution; and that just as life becomes manifest by the taking of forms, so by the breaking of form after form and the assuming of new ones, does life continually evolve. We see the life manifested in matter, drawing around itself matter which it appropriates as form. As form wastes in the exercising of life-functions, the life is ever engaged in drawing in fresh matter to replace that which has been lost. We see that the form is always decaying and always being renewed, and that the life can only find possibility of manifestation by thus taking fresh matter continually into its decaying form, and thus preserving it as the vehicle of manifestation; only by thus continually grasping after unappropriated matter, and appropriating it for the building up and renewing of its form, can life evolve.

Thus there comes to be implanted in the very nature of the growing being, the idea that by taking, by grasping, by holding, the life is preserved, the life is increased. This seems to be what the life is learning by its contact with matter, and it does not realise, in the earlier stages, that taking grasping, holding, keeping, is not really the condition of the life, but the condition of the maintenance of that form in which life is manifested. The form cannot continue to exist, but by virtue of the taking in of fresh matter. As the life goes on increasing, developing, this constant appropriation is the mark of the evolving Jîva. Everywhere is he learning, that in the path of Pravṛitti, the path of forth-going, he must grasp, take, hold and appropriate. Everywhere he is learning to try to absorb into himself other forms, and by union of other forms with his own to preserve the continuity of his existence in form.

When the great Teachers began to give lessons

to the evolving Jîvâtmâ, when he had reached the necessary point of materiality, then strange teaching came to him, contrary to all his preceding experiences. The Teacher began to say to him: "Life is preserved not simply by taking, but also by sacrificing that which you had already appropriated. It is a mistake to think that you can live and grow, simply by the appropriation of other forms into your own, simply by the absorption of the life around you, that your own may continue to exist. All the world is bound by a law of inter-dependence. All living things exist by virtue of mutual exchange, by the recognition of the fact of mutual inter-dependence. You cannot live alone in a world of forms; you cannot preserve your own form by the appropriating of others, without contracting a debt, which must be paid by the sacrifice of some of the appropriated object, for the maintenance of other lives. All lives are bound together by a golden chain, and that golden chain is the law of sacrifice, and not the law of grasping."

The universe emanated by an act of supreme sacrifice, and can only be preserved by the continual renewal of sacrifice.

Hear what Shrî Kṛiṣhṇa taught: "This world

is not for the non-sacrificer, much less the other, O best of the Kurus." [1]

Man then cannot even live in the world of forms, save as he performs acts of sacrifice. The revolving wheel of life cannot go on, unless each member, unless each living creature, helps to turn it by the performance of acts of sacrifice. Life is preserved by sacrifice, and in sacrifice all evolution is rooted.

In order that this new lesson might be taught in the correct way, we find the great Teachers insisting on acts of sacrifice, and showing that by virtue of these acts does the wheel of life revolve, that brings to us all good things. Thus we see established in the Hindu ritual, the well-known five sacrifices, which include in their wide circle the sacrifices which are necessary for the due maintenance of the lives of all the creatures in the world.

We are taught that our relations with the world invisible, with the Deva-world, can only be preserved by the sacrifice to the Devas, in which we recognise this inter-dependence. We give to them, they give to us, and thus nourishing one another, we reap the highest good. [2]

---

1 *Bhagavad-Gîtâ*, iv. 31.

2 *Bhagavad-Gîtâ*, iii. 11.

Then we learn the sacrifice, which is called the sacrifice to the Ṛiṣhis, the sacrifice to the wise, the sacrifice to the Teachers. That is the sacrifice of study, by the performance of which is paid one of our debts, by the performance of which an obligation is discharged. For by study we learn in order to teach, and thus we keep up the succession of knowledge, handing it down from generation to generation.

Then we learn that we must also pay the debt to the Elders, the sacrifice to the past, the sacrifice to the Ancestors, to the Pitṛis; recognising in that that as we received from the past, we must pay our debt by giving to the future.

Next we learn to pay our debt to Humanity. We are taught that we must feed at least one man every day. We know that the essence of that act is not in the simply feeding one poor man. In that man who is fed, the Lord of sacrifice is also fed; and when He is fed, all Humanity is fed in Him. Just as when Durvâsa came to the Pâṇḍavas in their exile, and the feast being over, demanded food where no food then existed, and the Lord of sacrifice Himself came and told the Pâṇḍavas to search for food, and one grain of rice was found, which He ate, and His hunger was satisfied, and in the satisfaction of His hunger, the great host of ascetics found themselves filled; so in the sacrifice to man. In the feeding of one starving beggar, He is fed who feels Himself in all, in every human life, and thus feeding Him in the shape of one poor man, we feed humanity itself.

Lastly we learn to sacrifice to animals. In the sacrifice to animals, in the two or three animals that daily we are bound to feed, we are feeding the Lord of animals in His animal creation, and by this sacrifice the animal world is maintained.

Such the old lessons given to young humanity, to teach it the form and essence of the sacrificial act. And we learn that the spirit of the law of the five sacrifices is far more valuable than the letter of the law; and we learn to extend to that spirit of sacrifice the recognition of the law of the obligation, of the law of duty. When the Law of Sacrifice is thus interwoven with and united to the Law of Obligation, then the next step is placed before the evolving Jîva.

You have learned to do some acts as acts of obligation. You now have to learn that the world is bound by action, save by such action as is sacrifice.[1] You must learn that looking for the fruit of actions binds us to the world of actions, and that

---

1. *Bhagavad-Gîtâ*. iii. 9.

if we would be free from such binding we must learn to sacrifice everywhere the fruit of action. "With such object, free from attachment, O son of Kuntî, perform thou action." [1]

That is the next step. It does not mean that some particular actions are to be separated from a man's scope of activity as sacrifices, but that all actions are to be seen in the light of sacrifice, by the renunciation of the fruit of action. When we sacrifice the fruit of action, we are beginning then to loosen the bonds of action which bind us to the world. For have we not read: "that with attachment dead, harmonious, his thoughts established in wisdom, his works sacrifices, all action melts away." [2]

The world is bound by karma, by action, save that action which is sacrifice. That is the lesson which begins to be breathed into our ears, as we approach the end of the Pravṛitti Mârga, as the time comes for turning homeward, for entering the path of Return, the Nivṛitti Mârga. When a man begins to renounce the fruit of action, when he has learnt to perform all his actions as duty, without looking for their fruit, then comes the critical time in the history of the evolution of the human soul;

1. *Bhagavad-Gîtâ*, iii. 9.
2. *Bhagavad-Gîtâ*, iv. 23.

then, as he is sacrificing the fruit of action, there sounds out to him a still higher note, a still higher lesson, which is to lead him over into the Nivṛitti Mârga, the Path of Return. "Better than the sacrifice of wealth is the sacrifice of wisdom, O Parantapa," says Shrî Kṛiṣhṇa. "All actions in their entirety, O Pârtha, are contained in wisdom. Learn thou this by discipleship, by questionings, and by worship. The wise, the seers of the Essence of things, will instruct thee in wisdom. And having known this, thou shalt not again fall into this confusion, O Pâṇḍava, for by this thou wilt see all beings without exception in the Self, and all in Me." [1]

There strikes out the note that we have learnt to recognise as the note of spirituality. By the "sacrifice of wisdom" we shall learn to see all beings in the Self, and thus in God. That is the note of the path of Return, of the Nivṛitti Mârga. That is the lesson which has now to be learnt by the evolving man.

The critical point comes now in the history of the evolving Jîva. He is trying to sacrifice the fruit of action, trying to be dead to attachments. And what is the inevitable result? The attachment to the fruit falls away, vairâgya seizes him, dispassion

1. *Bhagavad-Gîtâ*. iv. 34.

overcomes him, he finds himself hanging, as it were, in the void. All motive for action has disappeared. He has lost the stimulus of the Pravṛitti Mârga. He has not yet found the stimulus of the Nivṛitti Mârga. Disgust of all objects is upon him. He seems to have wearied of the Law of Duty; he has not yet seen the heart of the Law of Sacrifice. At this moment of pause, at this moment of suspension in the void, he seems to have lost touch with the world of forms and objects, but he has not yet found touch with the world of life, with "the other side."

It is as though a man, crossing from precipice to precipice by a narrow bridge, suddenly found the bridge yield beneath his steps; he cannot return, he cannot reach out to the brink beyond. He seems to be hanging in the void, in mid-air, over the chasm; he has lost touch with all.

Fear not, O trembling soul, when that moment of utmost isolation cometh. Fear not to lose touch with the transitory, ere thou findest touch with the Eternal. Listen to those who have felt the same isolation, but have passed beyond, who have found the seeming void to be a veritable fulness: hear them proclaiming the Law of Life, upon which thou hast now to enter: "He that loveth his life shall lose it, but he that loseth his life shall find it unto Life Eternal."

This is the test of the Inner Life. You cannot touch the higher until you have lost grasp of the lower. You cannot feel the higher, until the touch of the lower is becoming that of a corpse. A child climbing up a ladder against a precipice hears the voice of his father calling him from above. He wants to reach the father, but he is clinging close to the ladder with both hands as he sees the yawning gulf below. But the voice tells him: "Loose your grasp from the ladder and stretch your hands out above your head." But the child fears. If he looses his grasp of the ladder, will he not fall into the yawning gulf below? He cannot see above his head. The air seems empty, there is nought to grasp. Then comes the supreme act of faith. He looses grasp of his ladder. He stretches up his empty hands into the empty air above him; and lo! his father's hands have clasped his own, and the strength of the father uplifts him to his own side. Such is the Law of the Higher Life. In giving up the lower, the higher is secured; and by throwing up the life we know, the Life Eternal gains us as its own.

None but those who have felt it may know the horror of that great emptiness, where the world of form has vanished, but where the life of the Spirit is not yet felt. But there is no other way between the life in form and the life in Spirit. There between them stretches the gulf which must be crossed; and, strange as it may seem, it is in the moment of uttermost isolation, when the man is thrown back into himself, and there is nothing around him but the silent void, it is then that from out that nothingness of being the Eternal Being arises; and he who dared to spring from the foothold of the temporal finds himself on the sure rock of the Eternal.

Such the experience of all those who in the past have reached the spiritual life. Such the record they have left us for our encouragement and cheering when, to us too, this gulf presents itself for crossing. We read in the Shâstras and in those outer actions that are full of deepest meaning, that when the disciple approached his Teacher, he must ever come with sacrificial fuel in his hand. What is the sacrificial fuel? It represents *everything* that belongs to the life of form, everything that belongs to the personal lower self. All must be thrown into the fire of sacrifice, nought must be kept back. He must burn his lower nature, and his own hands must light the fire. He must sacrifice himself. None else may do it for him. Give then the life and surrender it utterly. Keep not back alive anything, so far as you know it; cry aloud to the Lord of the burning-ghât that the sacrifice is lying on the altar, and shrink not from the consuming fire. In the blankness of isolation, trust the Law which cannot fail. If the Law of Sacrifice be strong enough to uphold the weight of the universe, will it break beneath the weight of an atom like myself? It is strong enough to be trusted; it is the strongest thing there is. The Law of Sacrifice is that the life of the Spirit consists in giving, and not in taking, in pouring itself out and not in grasping, in self-surrender and not in self-appropriation, in utterly giving all that one has, sure that the fulness of the Life Divine will enter in. And see how natural it is. The Life inexhaustible is found, that is ever bubbling up out of the illimitable fulness of the Self. Form is limited, life is unlimited. Therefore the form lives by taking, and the life grows by giving. Just in proportion as we empty ourselves of all that we have, is there room for the Divine fulness to flow in, and fill us more than we were ever filled before. Therefore the note of the Nivṛitti Mârga is renunciation. Renunciation is the secret of Life, as appropriation is the secret of Form.

This then is the Law of Sacrifice that we must

learn. To give ungrudgingly, and ever again to give: by this and this alone we live.

On first entering the Nivṛitti Mârga, where Renunciation offers herself as our guide, her voice may seem cold and stern, her aspect may seem almost menacing. Trust her, none the less, whatever the outer appearance, and try to understand why sacrifice at first sight gives us the idea of pain.

From the standpoint of form, the aspect of sacrifice is the breaking up of forms, the throwing away of things; and the form, which feels the life withdrawing from it, cries out in its anguish, in its terror, towards the withdrawing life that maintains its very existence; and so we come to think of sacrifice as an act of pain, as an act accompanied with anguish and with terror, and this must be as long as we identify ourselves with the form.

But when we begin to live the life of Spirit, the life which recognises the One in the manifold forms, then there begins to dawn upon us the supreme spiritual truth, that sacrifice is not pain but joy, is not sorrow but delight, that that which to the flesh is painful is bliss to the Spirit, which is our true life. Then we see that the aspect of sacrifice that was sorrowful was an utter delusion, that keener than any pleasure that the world can give, more joyous than any joy that comes from wealth or position, more blissful than any bliss that the world can offer, is the bliss of the free Spirit, which, by pouring itself out, finds the union with the Self, and knows that it is living in many forms, flowing along many channels, instead of following the limitation of a single form.

Here is the joy of the Saviours of mankind, of Those who have risen to the knowledge of unity, and have become the Guides, the Helpers, the Redeemers of the race. Step by step, slowly and gradually, They have mounted upwards and upwards, they have crossed the Gulf of Nothingness that I have spoken of, and have found a footing on the other side. They have recovered the sense of the reality of life, and in the Gulf of Nothinness, in which They for a time seemed to have lost Themselves, They suddenly found Themselves above the world of forms. All forms as seen from that higher level are the vessels of one informing Life and Self. They have found with a sense of joy inexpressible, that the living Self can pour itself out into all the innumerable forms, and know no difference between form and form, but all as the channels of one Spirit.

That is why the Saviour of the world can help the race and strengthen His weaker brethren. Hav ing risen to that great height where all selves are known as one, the different forms are all His own. He knows Himself in each. He can joy with the joyful, and feel sorrow with the sorrowful. He is weak with the weak and strong with the strong—all are parts of Himself. Alike to Him the righteous and the sinful. He feels no attraction to the one, nor any repulsion from the other. He can see that in every stage the One Self is living, that Life which is Himself. He knows himself in the stone, in the plant, in the brute, in the savage, as in the Saint and the Sage, and He sees one Life everywhere and knows himself that Life. Where then is there room for fear, where then is there room for reproach? There is nothing but One Self, and nothing outside It either to fear or to challenge.

That is the true Peace, and that and that alone is Wisdom. To know the Self is alone the spiritual life, and that life is joy and peace.

Thus the Law of Sacrifice, which is the Law of Life, is also the Law of Joy, and we know that nothing has a keener pleasure than the pleasure of pouring out and not taking in, and that no limited joy can be equal to the joy of self-surrender.

Were it possible for each of us to catch for a moment a faint glimpse of the Spiritual Life, then the transitory world would assume its true proportions, and we should see the worthlessness of all that man accounts as precious. The Law of Sacrifice, which is the Law of Life and the Law of Joy and the Law of Peace, is summed up in this Mahâvâkya, this great Word; "I am Thou; Thou art I."

And now for a moment let us bring this lofty idea down to the level of our daily lives, and see how the Law of Sacrifice, in its working in ourselves, will manifest in the outer world of men.

We have learnt to realise, if but for a moment, the unity of the Self. We have learned a word, a letter, of the Book of Wisdom. How then shall we behave ourselves to our brother men? We see a man low, degraded, ignorant and foul. No special tie of kindred nor past karma binds us to him, nor does anything that we regard as obligation join our form to his. But, by the Law of Sacrifice, having realised the unity of the Self, when we see that outcast member of the human family, we see the Self in him, and the form vanishes, and we know that we are that man, and that man is ourself. Hence compassion takes the place of what in the man of the world is repulsion. Love takes the place of hatred, and tenderness replaces indifference, and the Sacrificer is marked in his attitude to those around him by this touch of divine compassion, which cannot see the repulsiveness of the outer form, but can only realise the beauty of the Self enshrined therein.

The Sacrificer comes across a man who is ignorant, while he himself is wise. Does he feel the contempt of the man of knowledge for the man of ignorance, and hold himself above him as his superior and as separate? Nay, he does not feel his wisdom as his own, but as common property belonging to all alike, and he shares his wisdom in the separate form with the ignorance in the other separate form: and he does it without feeling the difference, because of the unity of the Self.

And so with every other difference of the world of forms. The man who lives by the Law of Sacrifice realises the unity of the Self, and recognises only a difference in the containing vessel and not in the indwelling life; hence he only gathers wisdom and knowledge into his separate vessel for the sake of sharing what he gathers with others, and for others; and he loses utterly the sense of separate life, and becomes part of the Life of the World.

As he realises this, and knows that the only value of the body is to be a channel of the higher, to be an instrument of that life, he slowly and gradually rises above all thoughts, save the thought of unity, and feels himself a part of this great suffering world. Then he feels that the griefs of humanity are his griefs, the sins of humanity are his sins, the weaknesses of his brother are his weaknesses, and thus he realises unity, and sees through all differences the underlying One Self.

Only in this way can we live in the Eternal.

"Those who see differences pass from death to death;" thus speak the Shruti. The man who sees difference is really continually dying, for he is living in the form, which is decaying every moment and is therefore death, and not in the Spirit, which is life.

Just then, in proportion as you and I, my brothers, do not recognise the difference between each and each, but feel the unity of life, and know that that life is common to all, and that none has a right to boast of his share of it, nor to be proud that his share is different from the share of another, only thus and in that proportion shall we live the Spiritual Life.

That is the last word, it seems, of the Wisdom that the Sages have taught us. Nothing less than this is spiritual, nothing less than this is wisdom, nothing less than this is real life.

Oh! if for one passing moment, I could show to you, by any skill of tongue or passion of emotion, one gleam of the faint glimpse—that by the grace of the Masters I have caught—of the glory and the beauty of the Life that knows no difference and recognises no separation, then the charm of that glory would so win your hearts, that all earth's beauty would seem but ugliness, all earth's gold but dross, all earth's treasures but dust on the roadside, beside the inexpressible joy of the life that knows itself as One.

Hard to keep it, even when once seen, amidst the separated lives of men, amidst the glamour of the senses, and the delusions of the mind. But once to have seen it, though but for a moment, changes the whole world, and having beheld the majesty of the Self, no life save that seems worth living.

How shall we make it real, how shall we make it our own, this wonderful recognition of the Life beyond all lives, of the Self beyond all selves? Only by daily acts of renunciation in the little things of life; only by learning in every thought, word and action to live and love the Unity; and not only to speak it, but to practise it on every occasion, by putting ourselves last and others first, by always seeing the need of others and trying to supply it, by learning to be indifferent to the claim of our own lower nature and refusing to listen to it. I know of no road save this humble, patient, persevering endeavour, hour after hour, day after day, year after year, until at last the mountain tops are climbed.

We talk of the Great Renunciation. we speak of These, before whose Feet we bow, as Those who have "made the Great Renunciation." Do not dream that They made Their renunciation, when, standing on the threshold of Nirvâṇa, They heard the sobbing of the world in anguish, and turned back to help. It was not then that the real, the great, renunciation was made. They made it over and over again in the hundreds of lives that lie behind Them; They made it by the constant practice of the small renunciations of life, by continual pity, by daily sacrifices in common human life. They did not make it at the last hour, when on the threshold of Nirvâṇa, but through the course of lives of sacrifice; until, at last, the Law of Sacrifice became so much the law of Their being, that They could not do anything at the last moment, when the choice was Theirs, save register on the record of the universe the innumerable renunciations of the past.

You and I, my brothers, to-day, if we will, may

begin to make the Great Renunciation, and if we do not begin it in the daily life, in our hourly dealings with our fellows, be assured we should not be able to make it when we stand on the mountain crest. The habit of daily sacrifice, the habit of thinking, the habit of always giving and not taking, only thus shall we learn to make that which the outer world calls the Great Renunciation. We dream of great deeds of heroism, we dream of mighty ordeals, we think that the life of discipleship consists in tremendous trials for which the disciple prepares himself, towards which he marches with open vision, and then by one supreme effort, by one brave struggle, gains his crown of victory.

Brothers, it is not so. The life of the disciple is one long series of petty renunciations, one long series of daily sacrifices, one continual dying in time in order that the higher may eternally live. It is not a single deed that strikes the world with wonder which makes true discipleship, else were the hero or the martyr greater than the disciple. The life of the disciple is lived in the home, is lived in the town, is lived in the office, is lived in the market place, yea, amid the common lives of men. The true life of sacrifice is that which utterly forgets itself, in which renunciation becomes so common that there is no effort, that it becomes a thing of course. If we lead that life of sacrifice, if we lead that life of renunciation, if daily, perseveringly, we pour out ourselves for others, we shall find ourselves one day on the summit of the mountain, and shall discover that we have made the Great Renunciation, without ever dreaming that any other act were possible.

PEACE TO ALL BEINGS.